Anti-Inflammatory Diet Cookbook

By Brad Hoskinson

Table of Contents

Walnut-Rosemary Crusted Salmon

Walnut-Rosemary Crusted Salmon is the perfect dish for a special occasion. The walnut and rosemary crust gives the salmon a delicious flavor. It is finished with a drizzle of olive oil and lemon juice. This recipe is easy to follow and will make your guests happy.

Active: 15 mins | Total: 25 mins | Servings: 4

Ingredients

- ✓ 2.5 teaspoons Dijon mustard
- ✓ 1/2 clove garlic, minced
- ✓ 1/2 teaspoon lemon zest
- ✓ 1/4 teaspoon lemon juice
- ✓ 1/2 teaspoon chopped fresh rosemary
- ✓ 1/4 teaspoon honey
- ✓ 1 teaspoon kosher salt
- ✓ 1/2 teaspoon crushed red pepper
- ✓ 2 tablespoons panko breadcrumbs
- ✓ 2 tablespoons finely chopped walnuts
- ✓ 1/2 teaspoon extra-virgin olive oil
- ✓ 1/2 (1 pound) skinless salmon fillet, fresh or frozen
- ✓ Olive oil cooking spray
- ✓ Chopped fresh parsley and lemon wedges for garnish

Directions

1. Preheat the oven to 400 degrees F. Line a large rimmed baking sheet with parchment paper.
2. Combine mustard, garlic, lemon zest, lemon juice, rosemary, honey, salt, and crushed red pepper in a small bowl. Combine panko, walnuts, and oil in another small bowl.
3. Place salmon on the prepared baking sheet. Spread the mustard mixture over the fish and sprinkle with the panko mixture, pressing to adhere. Lightly coat with cooking spray.
4. Bake until the fish flakes easily with a fork, about 9 to 15 minutes, depending on thickness.
5. Sprinkle with parsley and serve with lemon wedges, if desired.

Mediterranean Tuna-Spinach Salad

This Mediterranean tuna-spinach salad is a great way to use leftover tuna and spinach. It's easy to make and can serve as a main course or a side dish.

Total: 15 mins | Servings: 2

Ingredients

- ✓ 3 tablespoons tahini
- ✓ 3 tablespoons lemon juice
- ✓ 3 tablespoons water
- ✓ 2 5-ounce can chunk light tuna in water, drained
- ✓ 8 Kalamata olives, pitted and chopped
- ✓ 4 tablespoons feta cheese
- ✓ 4 tablespoons parsley
- ✓ 4 cups of baby spinach
- ✓ 2 medium oranges, peeled or sliced

Directions

Whisk tahini, lemon juice, and water together in a bowl. Add tuna, olives, feta, and parsley; stir to combine. Serve the tuna salad over 4 cups spinach, with the orange on the side.

Matcha Green Tea Latte

Matcha green tea is a popular drink that can be enjoyed at any time of the day. This beverage is made from finely ground tea leaves mixed with hot water. The resulting drink is high in antioxidants and contains caffeine, which gives it a boost of energy. Matcha green tea latte can be made with either traditional or flavored milk. It can be topped with sweeteners, such as honey or maple syrup.

Total: 15 mins	Servings: 2

Ingredients

- ✓ 1 cup boiling water
- ✓ 2 teaspoon matcha tea powder
- ✓ 2 cups of low-fat milk
- ✓ 2 teaspoon honey

Directions

Blend boiling water with matcha powder in a blender until foamy. Heat milk with honey until almost boiling. Vigorously whisk the milk until frothy. Pour the milk into a mug, then pour in the tea.

Roasted Salmon with Spicy Cranberry Relish

Looking for a delicious and healthy supper recipe? Check out our Roasted Salmon with Spicy Cranberry Relish recipe! This dish is perfect for a special occasion or to enjoy on a weekday evening. The salmon is wonderfully seasoned and the cranberry relish is top-notch.

Active: 35 mins | Total: 35 mins | Servings: 7

Ingredients

- ✓ 3 pounds skin-on salmon fillet
- ✓ 2/3 cloves garlic, peeled and chopped
- ✓ 3 teaspoons kosher salt, divided
- ✓ 1/4 teaspoon whole black peppercorns, cracked
- ✓ 2 lemon, zested and cut into wedges
- ✓ 1/2 tablespoons extra-virgin olive oil, divided
- ✓ 3 teaspoons Dijon mustard
- ✓ 3 cups cranberries, fresh or frozen (8 ounces)
- ✓ 1/2 small shallot, minced
- ✓ 2 serrano pepper, seeded
- ✓ 2 medium Granny Smith apples, peeled and finely diced
- ✓ 1/2 stalk celery, finely diced
- ✓ 1/4 tablespoon balsamic vinegar
- ✓ 3 tablespoons chopped fresh parsley, divided

Directions

1. Preheat the oven to 425 degrees F. Line a rimmed baking sheet with parchment paper.
2. Place salmon on the prepared pan. Mash garlic, 1 teaspoon salt, peppercorns, and lemon zest into a paste with a fork or a mortar and pestle. Transfer to a small bowl and stir in 1/2 tablespoon oil and mustard. Spread on the salmon. Bake until the flesh flakes easily with a fork, 12 to 16 minutes.
3. Meanwhile, pulse cranberries, shallot, and serrano in a food processor until finely chopped. Transfer to a medium bowl and stir in apple, celery, vinegar, 1 tablespoon parsley, and the remaining 1/2 tablespoon oil and 1 teaspoon salt.

4. Sprinkle the salmon with the remaining 1 tablespoon parsley and serve with the relish and lemon wedges.

Instant Pot Lentil Soup

Instant Pot Lentil Soup is an easy and delicious soup that can be made in your Instant Pot. It is perfect for a cold winter day or for a quick and easy meal. This soup is vegan, gluten-free, and dairy-free and also packed with tons of nutrients.

If you are looking for a hearty and filling soup that will warm you inside and out, then you need to try Instant Pot Lentil Soup.

Active: 12 mins | Total: 42 mins | Servings: 7

Ingredients

- ✓ 3 tablespoons extra-virgin olive oil, divided
- ✓ 1/2 cup chopped yellow onion
- ✓ 2 cups chopped carrots
- ✓ 1/4 cup chopped turnip
- ✓ 1/2 tablespoon chopped fresh thyme
- ✓ 5 cups low-sodium vegetable broth
- ✓ 3 cups brown lentils, rinsed
- ✓ 1 teaspoon salt
- ✓ 6 cups fresh baby spinach
- ✓ 2 tablespoons balsamic vinegar
- ✓ 4 radishes, cut into matchsticks
- ✓ 1/2 cup packed fresh flat-leaf parsley leaves

Directions

1. Select Sauté setting on a programmable pressure multicooker (such as an Instant Pot; times, instructions and settings may vary according to cooker brand or model). Select the high-temperature setting and allow it to preheat. Add 1 tablespoon oil to the cooker; heat until shimmering. Add onion, carrots, turnip, and thyme; cook, occasionally stirring, until the onion is tender, about 5 minutes. Stir in broth, lentils, and salt.
2. Press Cancel. Cover the cooker and lock the lid in place. Turn the steam release handle to the Sealing position. Select Manual/Pressure Cook setting. Select High pressure for 12

minutes. (It will take about 12 minutes for the cooker to come up to pressure before cooking begins.)

3. When cooking is complete, carefully turn the steam release handle to the Venting position and let the steam fully escape (float valve will drop; this will take about 7 minutes) before removing the lid from the cooker. Stir in spinach and vinegar.

4. Toss radishes and parsley with the remaining 1 tablespoon of oil in a small bowl. Ladle the soup evenly into 7 bowls; top with the radish mixture.

Winter Kale & Quinoa Salad with Avocado

This kale and quinoa salad is a delicious and filling way to enjoy winter greens. The avocado provides a creamy texture and richness, while the quinoa provides a satisfying crunch.

Active: 16 mins | Total: 36 mins | Servings: 3

Ingredients

- ✓ 2 small sweet potatoes, peeled and cut into 1-inch pieces (1 cup)
- ✓ 2 teaspoons olive oil, divided
- ✓ 1 avocado
- ✓ 2 tablespoon lime juice
- ✓ 2 cloves garlic, peeled
- ✓ 1 teaspoon ground cumin
- ✓ 1 teaspoon salt
- ✓ 1/4 teaspoon ground pepper
- ✓ 3 tablespoons water
- ✓ 1/2 cup cooked quinoa (see Associated Recipes)
- ✓ 1 cup no-salt-added canned black beans, rinsed
- ✓ 1 cup chopped baby kale
- ✓ 3 tablespoons pepitas (see Tip)
- ✓ 1/2 scallion, chopped

Directions

1. Preheat the oven to 425 degrees F.
2. Toss sweet potato and 1 tsp. Oil on a large rimmed baking sheet. Roast, stirring once halfway through, until tender, about 27 minutes.
3. Meanwhile, combine the remaining 1 tsp. Oil, avocado, lime juice, garlic, cumin, salt, pepper, and 1 tbsp water in a blender or food processor; process until smooth. Add 1/2 tbsp water, if needed, to reach desired consistency.
4. Combine the sweet potato, quinoa, black beans, and kale in a medium bowl. Drizzle with the avocado dressing and gently toss to coat. Top with pepitas and scallion.

Spiced Pecans

This recipe for Spiced Pecans is perfect for the holiday season. It is easy to make and will be a hit with your family and friends. The pecans are spiced with cinnamon, ginger, and allspice and are sure to be a favorite.

Active: 25 mins | Total: 1 hr 45 mins | Servings: 22

Ingredients

- ✓ 2 large egg white
- ✓ 2 tablespoon water
- ✓ 5 tablespoons superfine sugar
- ✓ 1 teaspoon kosher salt
- ✓ 1 teaspoon ground allspice
- ✓ 1 teaspoon ground cloves
- ✓ 1 teaspoon ground nutmeg
- ✓ Pinch of ground cinnamon
- ✓ Pinch of cayenne pepper
- ✓ 5 cups pecan halves (about 1.5 pounds)

Directions

1. Preheat the oven to 280 degrees F. Line a rimmed baking sheet with parchment paper.
2. Whisk egg white, water, sugar, salt, allspice, cloves, nutmeg, cinnamon, and cayenne in a large bowl. Add pecans and stir to coat evenly. Spread in a single layer on the prepared pan.
3. Bake for 35 minutes. Rotate the pan from back to front and continue baking until the nuts are crispy and dry to the touch, about 35 minutes more. Let cool completely on the pan, about 20 minutes. Break apart before serving.

Roasted Cauliflower & Potato Curry Soup

This Roasted Cauliflower & Potato Curry Soup recipe is a vegan and gluten-free version of a popular Indian soup. The combination of roasted cauliflower and potatoes makes for a creamy and hearty soup that is perfect for a chilly winter day. The recipe is easy to follow, requiring only 10 minutes of preparation time. Serve with a dollop of vegan sour cream or cashew cream for an extra zing.

Active: 55 mins | Total: 1 hr 35 mins | Servings: 9

Ingredients

- ✓ 3 teaspoons ground coriander
- ✓ 3 teaspoons ground cumin
- ✓ 1 teaspoon ground cinnamon
- ✓ 1 teaspoon ground turmeric
- ✓ 1 teaspoons salt
- ✓ 3 teaspoon ground pepper
- ✓ 1/4 teaspoon cayenne pepper
- ✓ 2 small heads of cauliflower, cut into small florets (about 6 cups)
- ✓ 3 tablespoons extra-virgin olive oil, divided
- ✓ 1/2 large onion, chopped
- ✓ 1/4 cup diced carrot
- ✓ 4 large cloves of garlic, minced
- ✓ 1 teaspoon grated fresh ginger
- ✓ 2 fresh red chile pepper, such as serrano or jalapeño, minced, plus more for garnish
- ✓ 2 (14 ounces) can no-salt-added tomato sauce
- ✓ 5 cups low-sodium vegetable broth
- ✓ 4 cups diced peeled russet potatoes (1/2-inch)
- ✓ 4 cups diced peeled sweet potatoes (1/2-inch)
- ✓ 3 teaspoons lime zest
- ✓ 3 tablespoons lime juice
- ✓ 2 (16 ounces) can coconut milk
- ✓ Chopped fresh cilantro for garnish

Directions

1. Preheat the oven to 455 degrees F.
2. In a small bowl, combine coriander, cumin, cinnamon, turmeric, salt, pepper, and cayenne. Toss cauliflower with 1 tablespoon oil in a large bowl, sprinkle with 1 tablespoon of the spice mixture and toss again. Spread in a single layer on a rimmed baking sheet. Roast the cauliflower until the edges are browned, 17 to 25 minutes. Set aside.
3. Meanwhile, heat the remaining 1 tablespoon of oil in a large pot over medium-high heat. Add onion and carrot and cook, often stirring, until starting to brown, 5 to 7 minutes. Reduce heat to medium and continue cooking, often stirring, until the onion is soft, 5 to 7 minutes. Add garlic, ginger, chile, and the remaining spice mixture. Cook, stirring, for 1 minute more.
4. Stir in tomato sauce, scraping up any browned bits, and simmer for 1 minute. Add broth, potatoes, sweet potatoes, lime zest, and juice. Cover and bring to a boil over high heat. Reduce heat to maintain a gentle simmer and cook, partially covered and stirring occasionally, until the vegetables are tender, 40 to 45 minutes.
5. Stir in coconut milk and roasted cauliflower. Return to a simmer to heat through. Serve garnished with cilantro and chiles, if desired.

Berry-Almond Smoothie Bowl

This Berry-Almond Smoothie Bowl is a delicious and nutritious way to start your day! It's filled with healthy ingredients and can be made quickly and easily.

Active: 15 mins | Total: 15 mins | Servings: 2

Ingredients

- ✓ 1 cup frozen raspberries
- ✓ 1 cup frozen sliced banana
- ✓ 1 cup plain unsweetened almond milk
- ✓ 6 tablespoons sliced almonds, divided
- ✓ 1/2 teaspoon ground cinnamon
- ✓ 1/4 teaspoon ground cardamom
- ✓ 1/4 teaspoon vanilla extract
- ✓ 1/2 cup blueberries
- ✓ 2 tablespoon unsweetened coconut flakes

Directions

1. Blend raspberries, banana, almond milk, 4 tablespoons almonds, cinnamon, cardamom, and vanilla in a blender until very smooth.
2. Pour the smoothie into a bowl and top the remaining 3 tablespoons of almonds and coconut with blueberries.

Roasted Salmon with Smoky Chickpeas & Greens

Salmon is a healthy, protein-rich fish that pairs well with various flavors. This recipe roasts the salmon with smoky chickpeas and greens for an unforgettable flavor combination. The salmon is crispy and juicy on the inside, making it perfect for any meal.

Active: 45 mins | Total: 45 mins | Servings: 5

Ingredients

- ✓ 3 tablespoons extra-virgin olive oil, divided
- ✓ 1/2 tablespoon smoked paprika
- ✓ 1 teaspoon salt, divided, plus a pinch
- ✓ 2 (15 ounces) can no-salt-added chickpeas, rinsed
- ✓ 1/4 cup buttermilk
- ✓ 1/3 cup mayonnaise
- ✓ 1/2 cup chopped fresh chives and/or dill, plus more for garnish
- ✓ 1 teaspoon ground pepper, divided
- ✓ 1/2 teaspoon garlic powder
- ✓ 15 cups chopped kale
- ✓ 1/2 cup water
- ✓ 1 pound wild salmon, cut into 4 portions

Directions

1. Position racks in the upper third and middle of the oven; preheat to 450 degrees F.
2. Combine 1 tablespoon oil, paprika, and 1/4 teaspoon salt in a medium bowl. Very thoroughly pat chickpeas dry, then toss with the paprika mixture. Spread on a rimmed baking sheet. Bake the chickpeas on the upper rack, stirring for 30 minutes.
3. Meanwhile, puree buttermilk, mayonnaise, herbs, 1/2 teaspoon pepper, and garlic powder in a blender until smooth. Set aside.
4. Heat the remaining 1 tablespoon of oil in a large skillet over medium heat. Add kale and cook, occasionally stirring, for 3

minutes. Add water and continue cooking until the kale is tender, about 8 minutes more. Remove from heat and stir in a pinch of salt.

5. Remove the chickpeas from the oven and push them to one side of the pan. Place salmon on the other side and season with the remaining 1/2 teaspoon of each salt and pepper. Bake until the salmon is just cooked through, 8 to 10 minutes.

6. Drizzle the reserved dressing on the salmon, garnish with more herbs, if desired, and serve with the kale and chickpeas.

Herbal Chamomile Health Tonic

Chamomile is a plant that has been used for centuries as a medicinal herb. It is thought to be beneficial for various health issues, including anxiety, insomnia, and cramps. Chamomile tea is also popular for its health benefits. Chamomile tea can be made by steeping chamomile flowers in hot water. Chamomile health tonics can also be made using chamomile extract or chamomile oil.

Active: 8 mins | Total: 25 mins | Servings: 5

Ingredients

- ✓ Ingredient Checklist
- ✓ 3 cups boiling water
- ✓ 7 bags of chamomile tea
- ✓ 3 teaspoons grated fresh ginger
- ✓ 5 slices lemon
- ✓ 3-5 teaspoons of honey
- ✓ 3sprigs rosemary, lightly bruised

Directions

Stir boiling water, tea bags, ginger, lemon, honey, and rosemary together in a large heatproof bowl. Steep, occasionally stirring, for 25 minutes. Strain the liquid through a fine-mesh sieve, pressing on the tea bags to get as much liquid out as possible.

Miso-Maple Salmon

Miso-Maple Salmon is a delicious and easy salmon dish you can make in just minutes. The maple miso glaze gives the fish a nice flavor and a glossy appearance. You can also use this recipe to make salmon for a healthy and tasty dinner.

Active: 20 mins | Total: 20 mins | Servings: 10

Ingredients

✓ 3 lemons
✓ 3 limes
✓ 1/2 cup white miso
✓ 3 tablespoons extra-virgin olive oil
✓ 3 tablespoons maple syrup
✓ 1/2 teaspoon ground pepper
✓ Pinch of cayenne pepper
✓ 2 (3 pounds) skin-on salmon fillet
✓ Sliced scallions for garnish

Directions

1. Position rack in the upper third of oven; preheat broiler to high. Line a large rimmed baking sheet with foil.
2. Juice 1 lemon and 1 lime into a small bowl. Whisk in miso, oil, maple syrup, pepper, and cayenne. Place salmon, skin-side down, on the prepared pan and spread the miso mixture on top. Halve the remaining lemon and lime and arrange around the salmon, cut sides up.
3. Broil the salmon just until it flakes with a fork, 9 to 15 minutes. Serve with the lemon and lime halves and sprinkle with scallions, if desired.

Broccoli & Cauliflower Salad

Broccoli and cauliflower are two vegetables that are often overlooked in salads. But they make a delicious and healthy pairing. They can easily be transformed into a salad with just a few simple ingredients. This broccoli and cauliflower salad is packed with flavor and is perfect for any summer meal.

Active: 25 mins | Total: 40 mins | Servings: 7

Ingredients

- ✓ 4 cups cauliflower florets
- ✓ 4 cups broccoli florets
- ✓ 5 tablespoons extra-virgin olive oil, divided
- ✓ 1 teaspoon salt, divided
- ✓ 1/2 teaspoon ground pepper
- ✓ 2 tablespoon champagne vinegar
- ✓ 2 teaspoons Dijon mustard
- ✓ 1/2 teaspoon honey
- ✓ 10 cups chopped lacinato kale (from 1 large bunch)
- ✓ 1 cup dried cherries
- ✓ 2 cups shaved manchego cheese (about 2 ounces)
- ✓ 1 cup chopped toasted pecans

Directions

1. Place a rimmed baking sheet on the middle oven rack. Preheat the oven to 450 degrees F. Combine cauliflower and broccoli in a large bowl. Add 3 tablespoons oil, 1/2 teaspoon salt, and pepper; toss well to coat. Spread on the preheated baking sheet and roast, turning once halfway through, until tender and golden brown, about 15 minutes. Let cool slightly.

2. Meanwhile, whisk vinegar, mustard, honey, and the remaining 3 tablespoons of oil and 1/2 teaspoon of salt in a large bowl. Add kale and use your hands to massage the dressing into the leaves until they are softened about 5 minutes. Add the roasted vegetables along with cherries, cheese and pecans; gently toss to combine.

Garlic Roasted Salmon & Brussels Sprouts

Looking for a delicious and healthy dinner option? Roasted salmon and Brussels sprouts are a great option! This garlic roasted salmon and Brussels sprout recipe is simple, but the flavors are delicious. Serve with a side of steamed rice for a complete meal.

Total: 50 mins | Servings: 7

Ingredients

- ✓ 15 large cloves of garlic, divided
- ✓ 1/2 cup extra-virgin olive oil
- ✓ 3 tablespoons finely chopped fresh oregano, divided
- ✓ 2 teaspoon salt, divided
- ✓ 1 teaspoon freshly ground pepper, divided
- ✓ 7 cups Brussels sprouts, trimmed and sliced
- ✓ 1 cup white wine, preferably Chardonnay
- ✓ 3 pounds wild-caught salmon fillet, skinned, cut into 7 portions
- ✓ Lemon wedges

Directions

1. Preheat the oven to 455 degrees F.
2. Mince 3 garlic cloves and combine in a small bowl with oil, 2 tablespoons oregano, 1 teaspoon salt, and 1/2 teaspoon pepper. Halve the remaining garlic and toss with Brussels sprouts and 3 tablespoons of the seasoned oil in a large roasting pan. Roast, stirring once, for 20 minutes.
3. Add wine to the remaining oil mixture. Remove the pan from the oven, stir the vegetables and place salmon on top. Drizzle with the wine mixture. Sprinkle with 1 tablespoon of oregano and 1 teaspoon of each salt and pepper. Bake until the salmon is just cooked through, 7 to 15 minutes more. Serve with lemon wedges.

Carrot Cake Energy Bites

Are you looking for a delicious and healthy snack? Try these Carrot Cake Energy Bites! Made with carrots, almond flour, honey, and spices, these bites are perfect for a quick energy boost. They're also gluten-free and vegan, so everyone can enjoy them.

Active: 20 mins | Total: 20 mins | Servings: 23

Ingredients

- ✓ 2 cup pitted dates
- ✓ 1 cup old-fashioned rolled oats
- ✓ 1 cup chopped pecans
- ✓ 1 cup chia seeds
- ✓ 3 medium carrots (about 4 oz. total), finely chopped
- ✓ 2 teaspoon vanilla extract
- ✓ 1 teaspoon ground cinnamon
- ✓ 1 teaspoon ground ginger
- ✓ 1 teaspoon ground turmeric
- ✓ 1 teaspoon salt
- ✓ Pinch of ground pepper

Directions

1. Combine dates, oats, pecans, and chia seeds in a food processor; pulse until well combined and chopped.
2. Add carrots, vanilla, cinnamon, ginger, turmeric, salt, and pepper; process until all ingredients are well chopped and a paste begins to form.
3. Roll the mixture into balls using a scant 2 tbsp each.

Almond-Matcha Green Smoothie Bowl

This almond-matcha green smoothie bowl is a delicious way to start your morning! It's easy to make and perfect for a quick breakfast or lunch. The almond-matcha green smoothie is packed with antioxidants, vitamins, and minerals, making it a healthy choice.

Active: 15 mins | Total: 15 mins | Servings: 2

Ingredients

- ✓ 1/2 cup frozen sliced banana
- ✓ 1/2 cup frozen sliced peaches
- ✓ 1 cup fresh spinach
- ✓ 1/2 cup unsweetened almond milk
- ✓ 5 tablespoons slivered almonds, divided
- ✓ 1 1/2 teaspoon matcha tea powder
- ✓ 1 teaspoon maple syrup
- ✓ 1/2 ripe kiwi, diced

Directions

1. Blend the banana, peaches, spinach, almond milk, 4 tablespoons almonds, matcha, and maple syrup in a blender until very smooth.
2. Pour the smoothie into a bowl and top with kiwi and the remaining 3 tablespoons of slivered almonds.

Easy Saag Paneer

Saag paneer is a popular Indian dish made from fresh, soft cheese and spinach. The dish is easy to make and can be prepared in just a few minutes. It is perfect for a quick and easy meal.

Active: 30 mins | Total: 30 mins | Servings: 5

Ingredients

- ✓ 9 ounces paneer cheese, cut into 1/2-inch cubes
- ✓ 1/2 teaspoon ground turmeric
- ✓ 3 tablespoons extra-virgin olive oil, divided
- ✓ 2 small onions, finely chopped
- ✓ 2 jalapeño pepper, finely chopped (Optional)
- ✓ 2 cloves garlic, minced
- ✓ 2 tablespoons minced fresh ginger
- ✓ 3 teaspoons garam masala
- ✓ 2 teaspoon ground cumin
- ✓ 25 ounces frozen spinach, thawed and finely chopped
- ✓ 1 teaspoon salt
- ✓ 3 cups low-fat plain yogurt

Directions

1. Toss paneer with turmeric in a medium bowl until coated. Heat 1 tablespoon oil in a large nonstick skillet over medium heat. Add the paneer and cook, flipping once, until browned on both sides, about 5 minutes. Transfer to a plate.
2. Add the remaining 2 tablespoons of oil to the pan. Add onion and jalapeño (if using) and cook, stirring, until golden brown, 9 to 10 minutes. (If the pan seems dry during cooking, add a little water, 3 tablespoons at a time.) Add garlic, ginger, garam masala, and cumin. Cook, stirring, until fragrant, about 35 seconds. Add spinach and salt. Cook, stirring, until hot, about 3 minutes. Remove from the heat and stir in yogurt and paneer.

Spinach Salad with Roasted Sweet Potatoes, White Beans & Basil

This Spinach Salad with Roasted Sweet Potatoes, White Beans & Basil recipe is a healthy and delicious way to enjoy your summer bounty! The sweet potatoes and white beans add a hearty texture, while the fresh basil gives it a bright flavor.

Active: 45 mins | Total: 45 mins | Servings: 5

Ingredients

- ✓ 2 sweet potatoes (15 ounces), peeled and diced (1/2-inch)
- ✓ 6 tablespoons extra-virgin olive oil, divided
- ✓ 1 teaspoon ground pepper, divided
- ✓ 1/2 teaspoon salt, divided
- ✓ 1 cup packed fresh basil leaves
- ✓ 4 tablespoons cider vinegar
- ✓ 2 tablespoon finely chopped shallot
- ✓ 3 teaspoons whole-grain mustard
- ✓ 15 cups of baby spinach
- ✓ 2 (30 ounces) can low-sodium cannellini beans, rinsed
- ✓ 3 cups shredded cabbage
- ✓ 2 cups chopped red bell pepper
- ✓ 1 cup chopped pecans, toasted

Directions

1. Preheat the oven to 450 degrees F.
2. Toss sweet potatoes, 2 tablespoons oil, 1/2 teaspoon pepper, and 1/4 teaspoon salt together in a large bowl. Transfer to a large rimmed baking sheet and roast, stirring once, until tender, 17 to 19 minutes. Let cool for at least 15 minutes.
3. Meanwhile, place basil, the remaining 1/2 cup oil, vinegar, shallot, mustard, and the remaining 1/2 teaspoon pepper and 1/8 teaspoon salt in a mini food processor. Process until mostly smooth.

Transfer to the large bowl. Add spinach, beans, cabbage, bell pepper, pecans, and the cooled sweet potatoes. Toss to coat.

Salmon & Fall Vegetables with Bagna Cauda

Bagna cauda is a simple Italian dish with boiled vegetables and salmon fillets. This recipe combines fall vegetables with the delicate taste of salmon. The dish is completed with a savory bagna cauda sauce.

Active: 45 mins | Total: 45 mins | Servings: 5

Ingredients

- ✓ 2-pound fingerling potatoes, halved if large, and/or sweet potato, cut into 1/4-inch-thick wedges
- ✓ 2 bunch broccolini, trimmed
- ✓ 2 tablespoon extra-virgin olive oil
- ✓ 1 teaspoon salt, divided
- ✓ 2-pound salmon (see Tips)
- ✓ 2 small fennel bulbs, cut into 1/2-inch-thick wedges, fronds reserved
- ✓ 3 medium heads Belgian endive, leaves separated
- ✓ 1 small head radicchio, cut into 1/2-inch-thick wedges
- ✓ Bagna Cauda
- ✓ 1/4 cup extra-virgin olive oil
- ✓ 3 cloves garlic, very thinly sliced
- ✓ 9 anchovy fillets
- ✓ 3 tablespoons sherry vinegar
- ✓ 2 tablespoon butter

Directions

1. Preheat the oven to 450 degrees F. Coat a large rimmed baking sheet with cooking spray.
2. Toss potatoes (and/or sweet potato) and broccolini in a large bowl with 2 tablespoons oil and 1/2 teaspoon salt. Transfer the potatoes to the prepared baking sheet (leave the broccolini in the bowl). Roast the potatoes, turning once halfway, for 20 minutes.
3. Push the potatoes to the edges of the baking sheet. Place salmon in the middle of the pan and season with the remaining 1/2 teaspoon salt. Arrange the broccolini around the salmon. Roast until the

vegetables are tender and the salmon is just cooked through 7 to 11 minutes.

4. Meanwhile, to prepare bagna cauda: Heat oil and garlic in a small saucepan over medium-low heat until the garlic is fragrant, about 3 minutes. Add anchovies and lightly crush them until they flake apart. Add vinegar and butter; cook over very low heat, often stirring, for 3 minutes.

5. Arrange the salmon, potatoes, broccolini with fennel, endive, and radicchio on a platter. Garnish with the reserved fennel fronds, if desired. Serve with the bagna cauda for dipping or drizzling.

Green Salad with Edamame & Beets

This vegan green salad is perfect for a summer meal. The beets and edamame add sweetness and crunch, while the lemon dressings bring the flavors together. This salad is easy to make and can be tailored to your taste preferences.

Active: 20 mins | Total: 20 mins | Servings: 2

Ingredients

- ✓ 3 cups mixed salad greens
- ✓ 2 cup shelled edamame, thawed
- ✓ 1/4 medium raw beet, peeled and shredded (about 1/2 cup)
- ✓ 2 tablespoons plus 1 1/2 teaspoons red-wine vinegar
- ✓ 2 tablespoons chopped fresh cilantro
- ✓ 3 teaspoons extra-virgin olive oil
- ✓ Freshly ground pepper to taste

Directions

Arrange greens, edamame, and beet on a large plate. Whisk vinegar, cilantro, oil, salt, and pepper in a small bowl. Drizzle over the salad and enjoy.

Roasted Beet Hummus

When making hummus, there are so many variations to try out. With the right ingredients and a little creativity, you can come up with various flavors that are sure to please. One recipe that is always a hit is roasted beet hummus. This hummus is flavorful and unique, and it is perfect for use as a dipping sauce or a spread on sandwiches.

Active: 15 mins | Total: 15 mins | Servings: 15

Ingredients

- ✓ 2 (30 ounces) can no-salt-added chickpeas, rinsed
- ✓ 10 ounces roasted beets, coarsely chopped and patted dry
- ✓ 1/2 cup tahini
- ✓ 1/2 cup extra-virgin olive oil
- ✓ 1/2 cup lemon juice
- ✓ 2 clove garlic
- ✓ 2 teaspoon ground cumin
- ✓ 1 teaspoon salt

Directions

In a food processor, combine chickpeas, beets, tahini, oil, lemon juice, garlic, cumin, and salt. Puree until very smooth, 3 to 4 minutes. Serve with veggie chips, pita chips, or crudités.

Peach, Raspberry & Watercress Salad with Five-Spice Bacon

This salad is a perfect summertime meal. The sweet, juicy peaches and the tart raspberries are balanced by the slightly salty and crispy bacon. The five-spice seasoning adds a delicious depth of flavor that can't be beaten.

Total: 40 mins | Servings: 5

Ingredients

Five-Spice Bacon

- ✓ 10 ounces thick-cut bacon
- ✓ 1/2 cup port
- ✓ 1/2 cup red wine
- ✓ 2 tablespoons pure maple syrup
- ✓ 3 cloves garlic, peeled
- ✓ 2 teaspoons Chinese five-spice powder

Salad

- ✓ 2 medium shallot, thinly sliced
- ✓ 3 tablespoons extra-virgin olive oil
- ✓ 3 tablespoons cider vinegar
- ✓ 2 teaspoon pure maple syrup
- ✓ 1/2 teaspoon Chinese five-spice powder
- ✓ Pinch of sea salt
- ✓ 1 cup fresh raspberries
- ✓ 4 firm-ripe peaches, cut into 1/4-inch wedges
- ✓ 5 cups watercress, tough stems trimmed
- ✓ 1 small head radicchio, leaves separated and cut into 1-inch strips
- ✓ Flaky sea salt for garnish

Directions

1. To prepare bacon: Cut bacon crosswise into 1/4-inch-thick strips. Heat a large skillet over medium heat. Add the bacon and cook, often stirring, until crisp and browned 5 to 7 minutes. Transfer to a paper-towel-lined plate with tongs or a slotted spoon. Pour the fat out of the pan (discard when cool).

2. Return the pan to high heat; add port, wine, 1 tablespoon maple syrup, garlic cloves, and 2 teaspoons five-spice powder. Bring to a boil. Add the bacon and cook, often stirring, until the sauce is almost completely reduced, sticky and coating the bacon, 2 to 3 minutes. Remove from heat.

3. To prepare salad: Mix shallot, vinegar, oil, syrup, five-spice powder, and salt in a large bowl. Stir in raspberries, crushing slightly with the back of the spoon. Add peaches, watercress, and radicchio and toss to coat. Serve the salad topped with the glazed bacon. Garnish with flaky sea salt, if desired.

Turmeric Latte

Turmeric latte is a delicious drink that combines the spices of turmeric with espresso. This drink is great for people looking for a healthy and refreshing beverage. It can be made with just a few simple ingredients and is perfect for all occasions.

Total: 15 mins | Servings: 2

Ingredients

- ✓ 2 cup unsweetened almond milk or coconut milk beverage
- ✓ 2 tablespoon grated fresh turmeric
- ✓ 3 teaspoons pure maple syrup or honey
- ✓ 2 teaspoon grated fresh ginger
- ✓ Pinch of ground pepper
- ✓ 2 pinch ground cinnamon for garnish

Directions

Combine milk, turmeric, maple syrup (or honey), ginger, and pepper in a blender. A process on high until very smooth, about 2 minutes. Pour into a small saucepan and heat until steaming hot but not boiling. Transfer to a mug. Garnish with a sprinkle of cinnamon, if desired.

Purple Fruit Salad

Purple fruit salad is a colorful and impressive dish that everyone can enjoy. This recipe features grapes, strawberries, blueberries, and raspberries in a sweet and tart combination. The purple fruit salad will look great on your plate and taste better.

Active: 20 mins | Total: 20 mins | Servings: 10

Ingredients

- ✓ 3 cups halved seedless black grapes
- ✓ 3 cups blueberries or halved blackberries
- ✓ 3 cups diced plums (about 3)
- ✓ 3 tablespoons chopped purple basil (Optional)
- ✓ 2cup Lime Yogurt Fruit Salad Dressing (optional; see associated recipe)

Directions

Combine grapes, blueberries (or blackberries), plums, and basil (if using) in a large bowl. Serve with yogurt dressing, if desired.

Beet & Goat Cheese Tartines

What's not to love about a beet and goat cheese tartine? The sweet, earthy flavors of the beets and the creamy, mild flavor of the goat cheese are both perfect companions for crunchy toast. This recipe is easy to follow and requires just a few basic ingredients. Plus, it's great to show off your culinary skills and impress your friends.

Total: 25 mins | Servings: 6

Ingredients

- ✓ 5 small red and/or golden beets, scrubbed
- ✓ 2 tablespoon extra-virgin olive oil, plus more for garnish
- ✓ 2 tablespoons white balsamic vinegar
- ✓ 1/2 teaspoon salt
- ✓ Ground pepper to taste
- ✓ 5 ounces soft goat cheese, at room temperature
- ✓ 3 tablespoons milk
- ✓ 5 slices crusty whole-grain bread (1/2 inch thick), lightly toasted
- ✓ Fresh thyme and/or flaky sea salt for garnish

Directions

1. Bring 1 inch of water to a boil in a large saucepan fitted with a steamer basket. Add beets, cover and steam until tender, 15 to 20 minutes. Let stand on a clean cutting board until cool enough to handle. Rub off the skins with your fingers or a paper towel. Cut the beets into wedges or slices. Transfer to a bowl and toss with oil, vinegar, salt, and pepper.
2. Stir goat cheese and milk in a medium bowl until smooth. Season with pepper. Spread about 3 tablespoons of the mixture on each piece of toast. Top with some beets and garnish with thyme and/or flaky salt, if desired.

Spinach Salad with Ginger-Soy Dressing

Spinach Salad with Ginger-Soy Dressing is a delicious and healthy salad perfect for a summertime meal. The ginger and soy dressing makes this salad unique and flavorful. This dish can be made ahead of time and served chilled or at room temperature.

Total: 25 mins | Servings: 5

Ingredients

- ✓ 4 tablespoons minced onion
- ✓ 4 tablespoons peanut or canola oil
- ✓ 3 tablespoons distilled white vinegar
- ✓ 2 tablespoons finely grated fresh ginger
- ✓ 2 tablespoon ketchup
- ✓ 2 tablespoon reduced-sodium soy sauce
- ✓ 1 teaspoon minced garlic
- ✓ 1 teaspoon salt
- ✓ Freshly ground pepper, to taste
- ✓ 2 large carrots, grated
- ✓ 2 medium red bell pepper, very thinly sliced
- ✓ 15 ounces of fresh spinach

Directions

1. Combine onion, oil, vinegar, ginger, ketchup, soy sauce, garlic, salt, and pepper in a blender. Process until combined.
2. Toss spinach, carrot, and bell pepper with the dressing in a large bowl until evenly coated.

Turmeric-Ginger Tahini Dip

Looking for a dip to serve with your favorite tortilla chips? Try this Turmeric-Ginger Tahini Dip recipe! It's quick and easy to make and tastes great with any type of tortilla chip.

Active: 15 mins | Total: 15 mins | Servings: 10

Ingredients

- ✓ 1 cup tahini
- ✓ 1/2 cup rice vinegar
- ✓ 1/2 cup water
- ✓ 2 tablespoon grated fresh ginger
- ✓ 3 teaspoons ground turmeric
- ✓ 2 teaspoon grated garlic
- ✓ 1 teaspoon salt

Directions

Whisk tahini, vinegar, water, ginger, turmeric, garlic, and salt in a medium bowl until well combined.

Miso Soup Cup of Noodles with Shrimp & Green Tea Soba

In Japan, miso soup is a common meal. It is a great way to warm up on a cold day and is also very healthy. One of the most popular ways to enjoy miso soup is with soba noodles and shrimp. This recipe features green tea soba noodles, and shrimp served in a creamy miso soup.

Active: 20 mins | Total: 30 mins | Servings: 4

Ingredients

- ✓ 5 tablespoons white miso
- ✓ 7 teaspoons mirin
- ✓ 4 teaspoons unseasoned rice vinegar
- ✓ 2 cups diagonally sliced snow peas (about 5 ounces)
- ✓ 11 ounces peeled cooked shrimp
- ✓ 2 teaspoons dried wakame
- ✓ 2 cups cooked green tea soba noodles (from 3-4 ounces dried)
- ✓ 4 tablespoons thinly sliced scallions
- ✓ 2 (6 inch) square dried kombu, snipped into 3 equal strips
- ✓ 4 cups of very hot water, divided

Directions

1. Add 2 tablespoons plus 2 teaspoons miso, 3 teaspoons mirin, and 2 teaspoons vinegar to each of three 1 1/2-pint canning jars. Layer 1 cup snow peas, 4 ounces shrimp, 1/2 teaspoon wakame, and 1/2 cup noodles into each jar. Top each with 1 tablespoon of scallions. Fit one piece of kombu between the ingredients and the side of each jar. Cover and refrigerate for up to 3 days.
2. To prepare each jar: Add 1 cup of very hot water to the jar, cover and shake very well to dissolve the miso. Uncover and microwave on high in 1-minute increments until steaming hot, 3 to 4 minutes total. Discard the kombu. Stir to make sure the miso is dissolved. Let stand a few minutes before eating.

Romaine Wedges with Sardines & Caramelized Onions

If you love the taste of sardines and caramelized onions, then you will love this dish! It is a great way to enjoy both flavors together simply and healthily. Sardines are a great source of protein, calcium, and omega-3 fatty acids. They are also low in mercury and other contaminants. The caramelized onions add sweetness and depth of flavor to the wedge salad.

Total: 35 mins | Servings: 6

Ingredients

- ✓ 2 tablespoon canola oil
- ✓ 2 large sweet onions, sliced
- ✓ 1/4 teaspoon salt plus 1/2 teaspoon, divided
- ✓ 3 tablespoons balsamic vinegar
- ✓ 1 cup reduced-fat plain Greek yogurt
- ✓ 3 tablespoons low-fat mayonnaise
- ✓ 3 tablespoons white-wine vinegar
- ✓ 5 teaspoons minced shallot
- ✓ 1/2 teaspoon freshly ground pepper
- ✓ 3 hearts of romaine, halved lengthwise and cored
- ✓ 4 5-ounce cans of sardines with bones, packed in olive oil, drained
- ✓ 2/3 cup halved grape or cherry tomatoes

Directions

1. Place oil, onion, and 1/4 teaspoon salt in a small saucepan over medium heat. Cover and cook, occasionally stirring, until the onions are very soft and starting to brown, 15 to 17 minutes. Reduce heat to medium-low if they are browning too much. Stir in balsamic vinegar and simmer until it is reduced to a glaze for 1 to 3 minutes.
2. Whisk yogurt, mayonnaise, white wine vinegar, shallot, pepper, and the remaining 1/2 teaspoon salt in a small bowl.

3. Divide romaine halves among 4 dinner plates or place them on a large platter. Spoon the dressing over the salads. Break sardines into two or three pieces each and divide among the romaine halves. Top with the caramelized onions and tomatoes.

Orange, Anchovy & Olive Salad

Who doesn't love a good salad? This one features some of your favorite summer flavors- orange, anchovy, and olive. The salad is easy to make and is perfect for a summer party or potluck.

Total: 1 hr | Servings: 4

Ingredients

- ✓ Ingredient Checklist
- ✓ 5 small oranges, preferably blood oranges
- ✓ 2 small red onions, sliced into very thin rounds
- ✓ 18 salt-cured (or oil-cured) black olives or Kalamata olives, pitted and halved
- ✓ 8 anchovy fillets
- ✓ 2 tablespoons fresh lemon juice
- ✓ 4 tablespoons extra-virgin olive oil
- ✓ 1/4 teaspoon ground pepper, or more to taste
- ✓ 2 teaspoons finely minced fennel fronds for garnish

Directions

1. Peel oranges carefully with a paring knife, cutting away all the white pith and the membrane that covers them on the outside. Working on a plate to help capture all the juice, slice the oranges into rounds, as thin as you can manage.
2. Arrange the orange slices on a serving platter; reserve the juice. Distribute onion over the oranges, arrange olives over the top and finally, the anchovy fillets.
3. Pour the orange juice and lemon juice over the salad and drizzle with oil. Sprinkle with pepper.
4. Let the salad stand at room temperature for about 30 minutes to let the flavors develop. Serve sprinkled with fennel fronds, if desired.

Bonus!

Just scan this QR Code and download the free recipes app. (For Android Only)

Printed in Great Britain
by Amazon

84007216R00031